To our loyal customers over these past 10 years...

Thank you for creating a new product category for us – and customized books – in the world of promotional products. You are our family.

It is so gratifying to have found so many of you who share our passion for books and the tremendous, lasting value they provide.

THE BOOK COMPANY
SMART. EASY. BOOKS.

800-367-9388
www.thebookco.com

ASI 41010 PPAI 281850 UPIC BOOKCO SAGE 65718

ACKNOWLEDGEMENTS
These quotations were gathered lovingly but unscientifically over several years and/or were contributed by many friends or acquaintances. Some arrived—and survived in our files—on scraps of paper and may therefore be imperfectly worded or attributed. To the authors, contributors and original sources, our thanks, and where appropriate, our apologies.
–The Editors

CREDITS
Compiled by Dan Zadra & Kobi Yamada
Edited by Kristel Wills
Designed by Jessica Phoenix

ISBN: 978-1-932319-89-7

2nd Printing. 06 10   Printed with soy ink in China

HAPPY BIRTHDAY

COMPILED BY DAN ZADRA & KOBI YAMADA
DESIGNED BY JESSICA PHOENIX

COMPENDIUM
incorporated

CELEBRATE YOUR EXISTENCE!

WILLIAM BLAKE

THE BEST AGE IS THE AGE YOU ARE.

MAGGIE KUHN

RIGHT NOW IS A GOOD TIME.

UNKNOWN

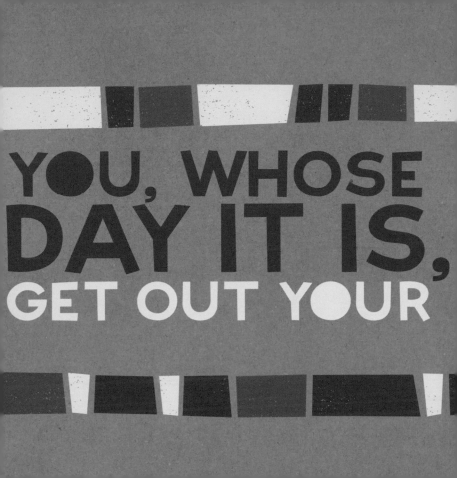

YOU, WHOSE
DAY IT IS,
GET OUT YOUR

RAINBOW COLORS
AND MAKE IT
BEAUTIFUL.

TRADITIONAL NOOTKA SONG

POP THE CORK
AND TIP THE
GLASS, AND
DRINK THE
MOMENT.

UNKNOWN

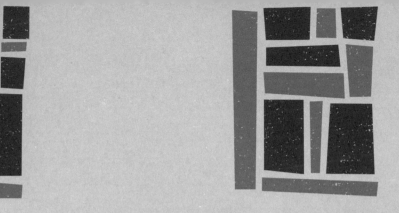

HOW BEAUTIFUL IT

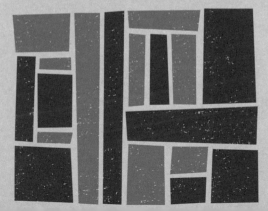

IS TO BE ALIVE!

HENRY SEPTIMUS SUTTON

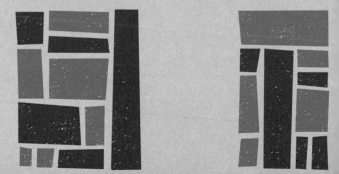

ALL THE GREAT
BLESSINGS OF
MY LIFE ARE
PRESENT IN MY
THOUGHTS TODAY.

PHOEBE CARY

OPEN YOUR MIND,
OPEN YOUR HEART,
OPEN YOUR ARMS,
TAKE IT ALL IN.

KOBI YAMADA

A POSSIBILITY WAS BORN THE DAY YOU WERE BORN AND IT WILL LIVE AS LONG AS YOU LIVE.

MARCUS SOLERO

EACH DAY COMES BEARING ITS OWN GIFTS. UNTIE THE RIBBONS.

RUTH ANN SCHUBACKER

AS YOU GROW OLDER, YOU'LL FIND THAT THE ONLY THINGS

YOU REGRET
ARE THE
THINGS YOU
DIDN'T DO.

ZACHARY SCOTT

ALWAYS BE READY TO HAVE THE TIME OF YOUR LIFE.

UNKNOWN

I WOULDN'T **MISS** LIFE FOR ANYTHING!

ANN WILSON SCHAEF

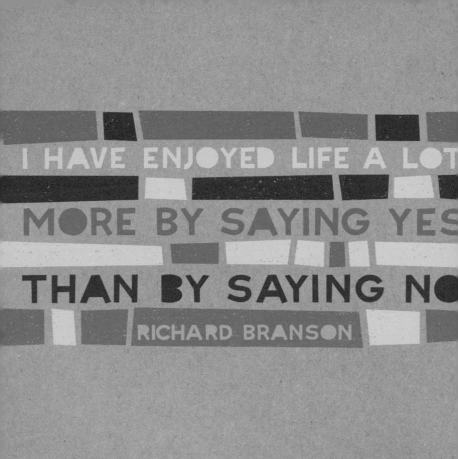

I HAVE ENJOYED LIFE A LOT MORE BY SAYING YES THAN BY SAYING NO

RICHARD BRANSON

A LIFE
SPENT
LOVING...
IS A LIFE
WELL
SPENT.

UNKNOWN

I HAVE FOUND THAT IF YOU LOVE LIFE, LIFE WILL LOVE YOU BACK.

ARTHUR RUBINSTEIN

A HEART THAT LOVES IS ALWAYS YOUNG.

PROVERB

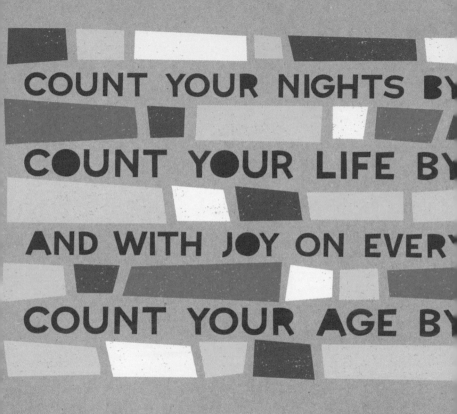

COUNT YOUR NIGHTS BY

COUNT YOUR LIFE BY

AND WITH JOY ON EVERY

COUNT YOUR AGE BY

STARS, NOT SHADOWS;

SMILES, NOT TEARS;

BIRTHDAY MORNING,

FRIENDS, NOT YEARS.

UNKNOWN

THE MORE YOU
PRAISE AND
CELEBRATE
YOUR LIFE,
THE MORE THERE
IS IN LIFE TO
CELEBRATE.

OPRAH WINFREY

ONE CANNOT HAVE TOO LARGE A PARTY.

JANE AUSTEN

THE LONGER
I LIVE THE MORE
BEAUTIFUL
LIFE BECOMES.

FRANK LLOYD WRIGHT

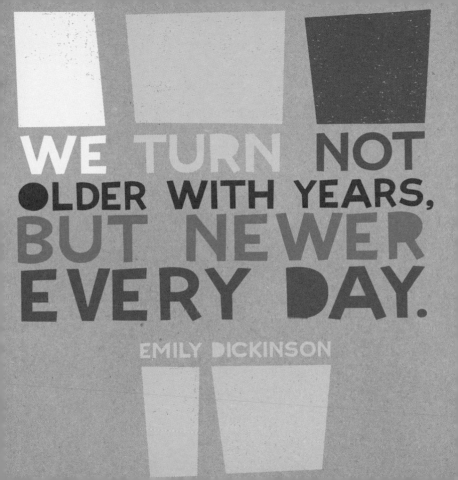

WE TURN NOT OLDER WITH YEARS, BUT NEWER EVERY DAY.

EMILY DICKINSON

DREAMS ARE RENEWABLE.
WHETHER YOU'RE FIVE OR 105,
YOU HAVE A LIFETIME AHEAD OF YOU.

DAN ZADRA

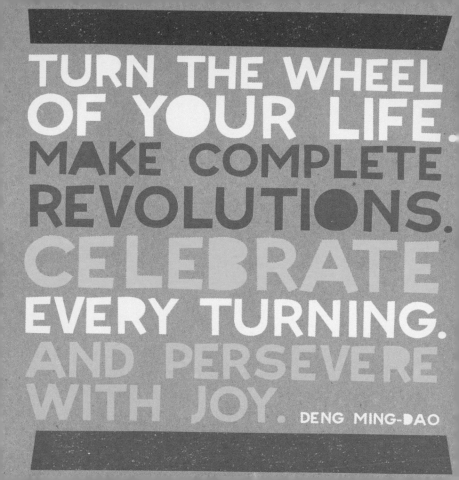

TURN THE WHEEL
OF YOUR LIFE.
MAKE COMPLETE
REVOLUTIONS.
CELEBRATE
EVERY TURNING.
AND PERSEVERE
WITH JOY. DENG MING-DAO

EACH BIRTHDAY
WILL BE A GIFT
OF TIME, AND
GROWING OLD
WILL BE A
GIFT OF LIFE.

UNKNOWN

...THE STRONGEST AND SWEETEST SONGS YET REMAIN TO BE SUNG.

WALT WHITMAN

AND THE SONG,
FROM BEGINNING
TO END, I FOUND
AGAIN IN THE
HEART OF A FRIEND.

HENRY WADSWORTH LONGFELLOW